LESSONS
IN
CONSCIOUSNESS

by

GARY LLAMA

OVOLR! / DEBACKLE
RICHMOND, VIRGINIA
USA

ISBN: 979-8-9909185-2-8

Gary Llama
Richmond, Virginia

For my great-uncle Ernest,
And YOU

Note:

For a while now, I have wanted to reprint a couple of books by my great uncle, Ernest S. Longest.

As you will read in here, I decided to make my own version, similar to the small book he self-released in 1964, here in Virginia.

He was a brilliant man and changed my life profoundly, more through his ideas, and more from reading them, than anything we experienced together.

If you would like to read them yourself, search for:

My Experience in Cosmic Conciousness, Longest, Ernest S, 1964
or
Meditation Techniques, Longest, Ernest S, Commonwealth Press, 1971

Explanation

This pamphlet / small book, is my attempt to distil the core of what has, for many years now, been my approach to living life. Inside, is a view of both spirituality, and morals and ethics that I believe to be true. And despite having written and published over a dozen other books previous to this one, this is the first time I have written about anything close to religion. And there is a reason for that.

I have always had a difficult relationship with the Christian Church, as a formal organization. Growing up as a Baptist, I had difficulty reconciling what I felt in my heart, with what I saw in the leadership, in the Church's operations, appearances, charity (or lack there of), positions on war, positions on capitalism, positions on poverty, and many other positions. I also, growing up in Richmond, VA, saw a very segregated lineage of Church, with White Churches, and Black Churches, and knowing the history the white churches had played in both slavery, and the racial terrorism of the Black community by so called, 'Men of God', during most of the time-line of America. Just the phrase, 'Man of God', or just 'Man', with its inference towards God, MEANT what later had to be described as White, to most white-skinned Europeans, so deep was their sickness of racial hatred.

And, I opposed the trinity of flag, God, and military, as was so usually displayed in much of the jingoistic messages I grew up hearing. And even today, the most religious of our population, are the same eager to fight its wars, a complication I saw at age nine when I decided that war was evil in God's eyes.

Also, I opposed the opposition to Gay-ness, Trans-ness, and anything different than the white, cis-gendered, male, essentially patriarchal point of view that dominates western Christianity, and somehow still dominates culture in certain parts of the country.

And above all, I cringed at the idea of putting anyone, above anyone. I saw the corruptness of clergy, the decadence of chapels, particularly compared to the lower wealth of it's congregation, as vile. And things like Protestant Ethic, and working till hands broken, for a reward from God later, seemed like the most sinister of ploys by the Kings who had been known to have re-written the Bible.

And then the idea that we should kneel before a God, pay service to him, worship him, dedicate our lives to him, seemed very much against everything I felt in my soul.

But I did feel the presence of God, of God's light, the entire time.

And with time and research, I learned every religion started off as pacifist. That the concept of 'Just War' itself came from power struggles between the Vatican and Kings, using the 'Just War' label as a way for the Church to hold on to some political power, something Kings would have to bargain with to have their populace fully accept the cause. And I learned of the most notable of Christians being against the idea that Race is anything more than a line we have carved across the colour of skin, and who believed we all were God's creation.

And with that, I began to explore again, and search deeper in myself, for those feelings felt so early on in life, and so constantly through my life, and a cause for good, I had been feeling since, around age 7 or 8, being given a card with my name, saying it meant 'Soldier of Light'. That was a war I could get behind.

Some of my friends have known this side of me, and by some, I mean MAYBE three at most. Mostly two. In the past year, more know.

But when I realized that even with something I have so proudly professed for myself, like Punk Rock, it is not in lack of criticism for the establishment or common form of it. I literally cringe at most things carrying that title, and again, could say the same criticisms I have had of Christianity, for punk: white, full of hypocrisy, justifying things that are notably against its birthing cause, and acting more like a club and business, than the reason folks came to it in the first place.

And finally, it is because a lot of this all seems fucking insane. There is a hard line right now between science and faith. To be a Christian means the assumption that you don't believe in evolution, or support the right to abortion, or believe in money, or Trump. But as a fairly scientific person, I have never seen a conflict between belief in God, and the theory of evolution, I see no conflict between God and being pro-choice, or between God and taking medicine. And personally, I think Donald Trump is a fucking charlatan.

So with that said, here are a collection of the things that I feel to be essential to the fairly happy life I have created for myself, which is immensely spiritual. It draws from Christianity, Buddhism, western new age... but it is all things I believe to be very true.

1. Let Go

You are already YOU.

The trick is to let go of who you THINK you are and who you would rather be, and to start embracing and loving your actual self.

This will require UNLEARNING external mechanisms, and unlearning the behaviours you think you need to do.

This is a process of aligning with the core of yourself and your own narrative.

The particular things you need to do in order to accomplish this are specific to you.

Follow your inner compass.

2. MAGIC

Anything we don't understand, seems to be Magical.

As Humans, we have evolved just enough to be able to survive and reproduce. Our EYES only see 0.0035% of the spectrum of radiation. Our EARS only hear a range of 20,000 frequencies on a spectrum that goes infinitely higher. We FEEL Time relative to, and slowed down by, the gravitational pull of the planet we stand on. In short, our ability of our senses is just good enough to live our lives. However, many things are occurring around us that we cannot perceive.

Occasionally, exceptional occurrences will become known to us, such as the way we connect with someone, or the ease at which an activity may come to us. These things can be seen to Magical. Take notice of them. Be thankful when you discover something for which you cannot explain.

These occurrences of results, many times more powerful than our effort, happen when we have aligned ourselves with our Path.

3. Path

If we observe a group of birds, their concerns and worries are not for the world in general, but rather for the interactions immediate to them. Our natural human tendency is to do the same. We are social beings, even those of us who are introverts. We can view the mood of the beings around us and feel its influence almost as powerfully as the weather. And with technology, we now have the ability to learn, receive updates, and worry about things very far removed from us. Accordingly, we must move through this world being mindful of what is, and what is not, on the path of life that is aligned with us.

For some of us, we may decide that our path is to try and heal a part of the world remote to us. For others, our energy may be more locally focused.

Finding the path that aligns better with your strengths and weaknesses, based on your own INTERNAL compass, will help to maximize your energy to give to the life you want to live, and die with.

4. Reflection

Reflection is the time in which we take the information we have accrued throughout our day, and think about what it means, relative to what we understand.

In this process, we challenge our previous understandings, and with that challenge, build our own truths: our own Knowledge.

Knowledge is not knowing facts. It is knowing the application of facts relative to our personal experience.

Knowledge then, is always personal and unique.

Developing this understanding, our Knowledge, and sharing it, increases the richness of the possibilities of knowledge in the world around us.

5. Love

Love is the strongest motivator in human existence. It's competitor, HATE, depends on love for its fuel. In fact, it could be argued that one cannot truly HATE without loving something. But HATE, is the energy of LOVE, clothed in disappointment, and aimed to obstruct blockages to LOVE through negative means. And in the process of using HATE, its dismissive and protectionist properties block the ability of a human to make knowledge and grow.

LOVE, however, is about letting light take its path. And accepting what shines in its path, as reality. And accepting these things for what they actually are. This does not mean condoning or agreeing with the things. But rather, simply accepting they exist. You cannot argue with shape of physical terrain, like a mountain. But you can figure out how to get around it. The obstructions we see may cause us to feel stress. But realize, that stress is directly related to our understanding of the work we must now do to overcome these obstacles on our path. And that work, IS in fact, our path. Accept the stress of this work, but do not let it darken your path.

6. Faith

Radiation energy penetrates everything in this world.

And the duration of Time, as we seem to understand it, is infinite.

And the elements that make us up at our core, never cease to exist.

So while our bodies will degrade, the things that make them up, will remain infinitely as part of this universe of particles.

With this understanding, we can see things like death, as simply the death of the body and the mind.

Ego longs for the persistence of these things, and depends on their permanence.

However, conscious energy, and the energy that animates each of us, has no start or stop date.

Worry for your death as you worried for your birth.

7. Mission

I believe we each have a mission. During our conscious life, we may begin multiple missions.

But it is critical to align yourself with the mission and fulfil it. Some folks believe they have a mission from a supernatural place. One could also make a purely evolutionary argument for a mission: that every person has evolved certain things at which they are good at, and the human race benefits most when these evolved abilities are employed. Think of what this world would be like, if the folks that made the art that touched us, or employed their knowledges of science to make the technology we depend on, or those whom touched us through their words or actions.. imagine if they had tried to take a path other than the one they took, and we never felt the almost magical things they shared with the world. That dim picture of reality should serve as the baseline of what NOT to do with our lives.

When you align with your better qualities, and use your unique skills to hone them, the direction of our individual mission tends to become very clear.

8. Feel

We must learn to navigate life by Feel. Some call it 'gut instinct', others, intuition. But I think both are the result of our bodies internalizing our Knowledge, into responses. And many times, our bodies will react before our minds can name and alert us to the particulars of an occurrence or discrepancy.

Learn to trust what you Feel. It feels different than anxiety, and feels different than worry. In me, it feels as a gentle nudge, that if explored, is actually as solid as anything I have ever felt.

Trust navigating by Feel and learn to discern it, and navigate your entire life upon it.

The very action of me writing this book was based entirely upon my faith in a gentle nudge.

My Experience

I grew up feeling a light inside me. That light felt noble, and good. As events unfolded through my life, I found myself almost serendipitously in place to be of service in moments where that light could help others. And from a very early age, I knew I would always be OK. Any fear I felt, was only for the work I knew would be required of me to reach the next step of my life.

Why did I feel this? I'm not really sure, but have a few ideas. One, when I would encounter things from the spiritual realm, like ceremonies, in churches, at funerals... anywhere where the human spirit was being worked more in accordance with the light and hope we have inside of each of us, I would feel that energy, with reverence in my bones. At funerals, where desperation had worn down the bodies of those morning, I could feel the light abounding in multitudes. And in each situation, I knew my place: to stand as a steward to those who could not stand. To use my strength in those times to help others find their own strength. That has been a mission I have been on for a very long time. The main duty in that mission is to hear folks fears, and redirect them towards the light, which is so obvious to me.

Why is it so obvious to me?

As a kid, I met my great uncle, Reverend Ernest S. Longest. He was from a generation very different from mine, and in first appearances, seemed to be as stuffy and devoid of interesting things, as most elders would appear to a kid. But these were appearances. In his day to day life, he was a Baptist minister, turned minister of metaphysics, whom in the 1960s, began self-publishing books from a press here in Virginia, to share the knowledge he had gained from his own spiritual journey.

His 1964 book, 'My Experience in Cosmic Consciousness', began like this:

"When the people flocked to Jesus to be healed and to be helped in other ways, he knew that he could not remain constantly with them for if he did so, they would fail to turn within themselves to find the indwelling Light of God, the Holy Comforter. So he left them.

It is not simply a matter of being able to heal someone, of lifting him up into a perfect body, or harmonizing him in other ways. What we must do is unfold our own consciousness into the Christ Consciousness, which already dwells within each of us, waiting for recognition."

When I first read this, as a early teen, I was turned off, but also intrigued. Turned off, because while I felt the light at so many church gatherings, I was disgusted by the behaviour of those around this light. It was as if they could not see it themselves. I was disgusted by the mundane sermons given around such beauty, and sometimes, such outright suffering. I saw it as disconnected, dishonest... how could these folks be around such beauty, in the presence of such power, and yet, show so little personal effect? Where they just USED to it?

In time, I came to understand that many folks do things because they THINK they should. And so while their path had arrived them at the church that morning, and their senses had given them cue that something Holy was occurring, perhaps they could not see what I was seeing. Which also made sense, because they were not acting as how I was acting. After church, they would return to their very uninspired, very decimated and oppressive lives, as if they had not just seen the light of the universe burst from a room as I had.

In time, I came to understand that ALL the worlds religions preached the same thing, to the same God. That the stories had been localized to time and place. The occurrence of prophets, localized to time and place. Humans are social beings, the perception means a lot. So sending a prophet, one must send one that will socially be accepted. Hence why no religions have a story about the prophet being a parakeet: we are already grasping at the edge of accepted sanity with these stories that challenge our understanding of the world, and even with human prophets, many will be locked up, killed, shamed, and exiled as mentally ill, or later, possessed, for seeing something humans have not yet decided to accept, en mass.

At a certain age, my mom shared something Ernest had told her, stating that to effect: Jesus, Mohammed, The Buddha, were all part of the same thing. All real. All carrying the same message. All working for the same God. And when we think of how many times these stories pop up through history, from such different places in the world, from such different cultures, it is amazing that the core is such the same.

Ernest wrote about it in a benediction from that same book..

"May He who is the Father in Heaven of the Christians, Allah of the MOhammedans, Jehovah of the Jews, Ahura Mazda of the Zoroastrians, Spirit of the Hindus, grant unto all Peace and Blessing. Peace, Peace, Peace be unto us and unto all living beings. And now, may the Blessings of the Universal Light of us all be upon this message as it is given to the world. Amen."

It was reading this benediction last night, that prompted this book your reading now to be written. Exaclty 60 years after his was self-published from Virginia, mine will be as well. I had never understood the benediction, or the power of it, until last night, the day of a total solar eclipse for some near Virginia on earth, I was talking to a friend who was in her own search for meaning and path to light. And in that, I was trying to help her in any way I could. And in our conversation, I began sensing that this book may be helpful, so I pulled it out, and began sending pictures of some of the pages to her, as she had for the book she was reading earlier. And in doing so, the power of the parts quoted here, resonated with me in a way they had never before. Passages I had read and considered many times before in my life, suddenly seemed indefensibly true, because they had finally lined up with where I was in my own journey, the way a song may, or a piece of art. It hit where it was meant to hit.

And in showing this to her, I realized that what I needed to share here, was that the light was inside of her already. Earlier in our conversation, she had shared pictures of the text of the book SHE was reading, and I was reminded of why I have generally avoided western Christianity, despite knowing it is of the same branch in which I believe: it was all external. It was using the body as a vessel, work as a means, to SERVE God, a model created in a time where Christian scriptures were re-written ad-infinitum by Kings whom the model of servitude best suited. The idea of God's light emanating from peasants, broken from toiling endlessly for the kingdom under an oppressive class system would serve only to illuminate the disparity and inhumanity of serfdom and monarchy, and the illegitimacy of these powers under the power of the light of God. To keep looking outside of ourselves, we are tricked to never find the power and the peace that is within us. Rather, to quiet our mind. To quiet our ego. To quiet our anxiety and judgement, and just allow ourselves to feel the good that ALWAYS runs through us... the GOOD, the GOD that runs through us, will emancipate us from the journey of discovery, and allow us to begin the journey of healing, and alignment.

And in the conversation, something else struck me. The text was searching for the meaning of Christ's resurrection. And in just reading it, the meaning became so obvious: It was simply that Christ had become a man, just like you and me, with God's light, inside of him. Just like you and me. The resurrection, was just to prove the doubters, and probably to avoid a religious belief focussed to squarely on Death, as it wasn't the point. The point was Christ became a man, and did every action of Christ, from the body of man. The same as you and I could. And it is in the externalization of that story, the deification, that we alienate ourselves, again, from our own potentials. Are we not the creations of our Creator? If we are, then we are certain to bear it's DNA, and evolve and shape ourselves as the DNA of the creator would allow. Much like we put the lives of other prophets on a pedestal, Martin Luther King, Gandhi, Mother Theresa.. in doing so, we learn to think of them as other, their powers unattainable. Their entire being magical. Rather than these lives being conducted from, what we have seen, is the same Christ-like body. The body of Christ was the body of Man. And the energy in him, is the light of God.

www.ingramcontent.com/pod-product-compliance
Lightning Source LLC
Chambersburg PA
CBHW030528130626
46549CB00007B/3153